Lauria/Frasca Poetry Prize 4

Sunset Cue

SUNSET CUE

Poems by Angie Macri

BORDIGHERA PRESS

All rights reserved. Parts of this book may be reprinted only by written permission from the author, and may not be reproduced for publication in book, magazine, or electronic media of any kind, except in quotations for purposes of literary reviews by critics.

© 2022, Angie Macri

The cover features *Early Morning Ascent* by Melissa Gill, relief print and shibori dye on fabric, 24" x 30".

Library of Congress Cataloging-in-Publication Data

Names: Macri, Angie, author.
Title: Sunset cue / poems by Angie Macri.
Description: New York : Bordighera Press, 2022. | Series: Lauria/Frasca poetry prize ; 4 | Summary: "The poems collected in "Sunset Cue" have a rare, mystical quality. Through her observant eye, love of science and nature, and poetic alchemy, Angie Macri transmutes her subjects-red-winged blackbirds, a garden at the end of fall, children at play-from the physical into the metaphysical"-- Provided by publisher.
Identifiers: LCCN 2021055831 | ISBN 9781599541822 (paperback)
Subjects: LCGFT: Poetry.
Classification: LCC PS3613.A28333 S86 2022 | DDC 811/.6--dc23/eng/20211118
LC record available at https://lccn.loc.gov/2021055831

Printed with Ingram Lightning Source.

Published by
BORDIGHERA PRESS
John D. Calandra Italian American Institute
25 W. 43rd Street, 17th Floor
New York, NY 10036

Lauria/Frasca Poetry Prize 4
ISBN 978-1-59954-182-2

TABLE OF CONTENTS

I

Sunset Cue	13
Marcescence	14
Trailing Point	15
Iron Is Red When You Put Water on It	16
While the wren sings, the heron flying across the lake	17
Stadium Effect	18
Star Witness, a Moth	19
Conclave	20
Grass Domes	21
Breakers	23
In the Labyrinth of the Smallest Bone	24
Dame's Rocket	25
Breaking the Horizon to Green Behind Her	26
Stained Glass	27
The Steel My Father Sharpened	28
At the East of the Garden	29
Grandchildren of Other Summers	30
Purple String	31
Don't leave. Stay here forever, said the father	32
All One	34
And Hope to Die	35
Particle, Little Part	36
Of the Air	37
American Robin	38
Marigold	40
Oh Be a Fine God, Kiss Me	41
First the Bats, Then the Stars	42
Morphology	43
Quartz Crystal	44
A Cameo Cut in Shell	46
Charm, Company, Trembling	47

II

Story	51
Enthalpy	52
Catoptromancy	53
Green Snake	54
In the city where a woman studies wings,	56
La donna è mobile	57
Equal Shine	58
Witch Hollow Road	59
Rowing in Eden	60
Maidenhair	62
So Eden sank to grief	63
A Good Pair of Scissors, if Taken Care of, Will Last You Forever	64
Graeae, What We Share	65
Before the Garden Door, Shimmering Light	67
Still Life with Apples	68
Another Man Who Lost His Head	69
The galaxy hung between the girl and her mother	70
Everything will be splendid: the grandmother will not drink habitually	71
Elegy	72
Learning Latin in Sparta	73
Raptor	74
Snake, Not Serpent; Hopelessness, Not Despair	75
Waterweed	76
NOTES	77
ACKNOWLEDGMENTS	79
ABOUT THE AUTHOR	81
ABOUT THE COVER ARTIST	83

for my grandparents,
Opal and Harlan,
Rocco and Angelina

I

Sunset Cue

It is the tyrant's custom to wear the sun under his wings,
to show the sun when challenged
in the pulse of aerial
display. His tail cuts,
not as the state cut the route

through the forest between the city and dam
but as space cut and come together
without a seam,
the kind of cut that heals
itself without a scar,

absolute rule which he reveals.
He sits on the road signs (for curves, for speed,
use caution please)
in his territory, his mate
lining a nest with cigarette filters

from the shoulders of the highway.
The ore in this place
has made man a king.
Like law, like ore, a sun
fits under the flycatcher's wings.

Marcescence

The garden still held flames into winter
but in a way no one remembered.
They didn't see brown as part of fire
in the oak leaves hung in angles.
Shouldn't they all have come down by now?
people asked each other, ready to burn
or bag them or blow them down storm drains.
In rain, the shade of the leaves deepened
as a signal. The air moved through them,
and the angels. Wrens worked around houses
while children watched them. Another pine
turned orange from the damage the beetles
were doing until it died, then stood until it fell.
People left the trees where they lay.

Trailing Point

The girls bend
to play in the ditch in evening,
the sun still enough
to be hot, tongues reaching
from an open oven.
Emeralds have melted
into blades
they pick to draw
through the water,
soft but yet sharp enough to slice
a finger or palm, a cut
that feels large
though it's small. They call
to each other to look
as they take turns dropping heads
off white clovers
into the pool.
They braid the stems.
They search for luck
and, not finding it, make
their own with mud,
fixing one leaf to the three.
Why is four lucky?
one asks the other,
who shrugs. Their bodies
cast skyscrapers behind.

Iron Is Red When You Put Water on It

The child has stained the back of her shirt again
with what looks akin to blood,
maybe mud, she says, from running, or red off the chain
from the swings. Her mother sprays the marks
and washes the shirt a second time
in hopes they'll fade.
She knows what it means to run so hard
to kick the earth free.
It must have clung to the child's shoulder blades,
where your wings should be, she tells the child
as she studies the girl's spine
to see if it's growing straight. She says nothing
about that, but this child wasn't born yesterday. She's seen
her brother's x-ray. Her mother rubs the cotton
and the child says sorry
and thinks ahead to tomorrow:
if she will be fast enough to get a swing,
if the ground will be dry enough
after another day of rain for the school to let them out,
if her mother will remember to trim her nails. She hopes not
because she cuts them close as if she wants
no dirt under them at all. That's right,
her mother says, why
didn't you remind me? Even the rocks
on the ground hold red like her body,
mud a memory of dust on her shoes and the god's mouth
where he bent to breathe to make a copy
of his form. The chains have been weeping iron
from all the rain.

While the wren sings, the heron flying across the lake

touches the water with one wing, deliberate
or a miscalculation, no way to say. The water
isn't deep except at the center, old creek bed
dammed to control flooding and create this,

pine water, needled water, lake of old bruises
blooming as old blood turns shades, absorbing
back into the skin. A car has parked in the woods
below the causeway. No need to speak with music

playing and what is there to say anyway? A secret, arms
warm back in their sleeves. Only the male wren sings
and must even in winter to defend his territory.
He repeats teakettle, teakettle: the water on the stove
is boiling, how can you ignore the scream? Around the car,
even the branches of the elms have wings.

Stadium Effect

One hurricane quickly followed another
until no one paid attention,
losing roofs common
even for prime ministers,
glass broken and flying, breaking again
to become even smaller
as it worked on returning to its origin.

In the states, people filled with sorrow
for where they'd just vacationed.
On a playground, a girl
began turning. I am the eye,
she shouted, knocking her friends down.
They demanded their own turn
until three or four were spinning

at the same time, laughing. Their legs
brightened with dust
as it hadn't rained in forever,
which meant no indoor recess,
the teachers sighed in relief.
Each one of the children
was screaming their name.

Star Witness, a Moth

The girl bends over sight words on cards
in red and yellow paper laminated
so it can't be torn, what she plays as a puzzle
on the coffee table.
                        The night is dry moss
in late summer, no longer
unexpected. The girl arranges evening
while the moth, a star at the window, beats
against the rhythm
                      of her speaking,
refrain, black and blue witness.
Father and brother pause to reread the sentence
she has assembled while humming
the dark blue moss,
                    what was breathing.

Conclave

This winter, there are so many cardinals
the woods can't hold them. They overflow the roads
and railroad crossings like flames a child
is criticized for drawing: shouldn't fire be orange or yellow,
maybe some combination? Yet she continues,
tongue between her lips pressed with the same pressure
as her fingers across the desk on the paper.
Time was, her mother has told her, cardinals were collected
and sold north as songbirds. The child's classroom
can be locked, can be barricaded, we'll throw pencils, scissors.
Weekends, the cardinals fly in front of them, sudden out of forests
that hold the shades of ashes,
their bodies even more vibrant because the sun
hasn't been out for weeks although it never rains or snows.
Females an old bruise on fire,
males red fire completely, they move as the path a sword
is cutting. With such a big box of crayons,
there are so many more choices like orange-red, and red-orange: side
by side, can't you see the difference?
Why would you ask for one named blood?
They sang better, her mother has read, if captured
rather than born in captivity.
No one is left alive that remembers.

Grass Domes

Having inherited
lavender suns
and blue moons
from volcanoes
and forest fires,

I prepared her crib
with cotton
and hopes, with a black
and white mobile
of triangles, circles,
squares that locked
together like sky
to tops of swamp oaks.

Ovenbirds eat crickets,
aphids, moths off leaf litter
on the forest floor
and line their nests
with hair, guarding
their wreathed eggs
in grass domes. Believe
that I took as much care.

She is my heir,
and my time revolves
around her heart,
which, as she came
six weeks early, beats
either too fast or slow.
Black rectangle leads
record her rhythms.

Water first to quench
the thirst, then ending
with cream, I give her
anything, my hours,
my light, my meter.

Breakers

He arrives in the water
where it breaks on the beach
marrying morning stars
to his feet.

Shadows, wind, pearls, souls,
I tell him stories in waves
of words. He holds close,
unsure in the face

of the giant sea. Under
the names of sailors, soldiers,
saints from my grandfather's world
of swordfish

and lamb, caciocavallo
and cuzzupe di Pasqua,
the flowers of zucchini,
how can my son

stand? Less than one, he does,
sun on sand and azure
roaring, dolphins an arm's
throw away.

He calls my hair water,
and he looks to where
the gulf swells, unwinding
from the sky.

In the Labyrinth of the Smallest Bone

The children in rows waiting outside
standard brick schools for their parents
know how long it takes a voice to reach
the ear in terms of canals and nerves.

My son tells me he can't hear God, and also
that the moon likes a dark room, and that
he might like to ask questions about God
in the middle of the night, and can he wake me.

So he joins me in the labyrinth
of the smallest bone pushing on a window,
the hollows of dawn, of query. The man's
in the moon tonight, adults used to say.
I never saw him there but would agree.

When I grew up, I saw him then,
a common man, and learned his mood,
the rule, his expression that said nothing of all
he had seen. Are there ghosts? my son asks.
Only in dark castles far away from us.

Our membranes tune in the stretch
of moonstrung blue, before the paper runs
but after the trains by the river, when the crickets
and ditch frogs are also murmuring.

Dame's Rocket

She arrives in the water
that runs off our roof
in this hard rain. The sound
boils up inside so that

I can feel it in her back
before I hear her laughing,
like grapes each laugh,
like bulbs of lung that send

air out and clench the new
with joy and comprehension.
In my arms, rain becomes
her universe rising into sense.

The dame's rockets hum
sweet summer nights,
their petal claws and corollas
purple along rails and in thickets.

Brought here from Europe
long ago, this is their home now,
like us, mothers and daughters
back to the first ones born

in bluebells of wilderness
and close rain that infuses all.
My cells' energy is hers
and will be in her children, too,

an atlas to the past like chains
of ferns with fronds,
fiddleheads, and sori
underneath for the next of us.

Breaking the Horizon to Green Behind Her

Shall I show you the mermaid
in a blue sea under yellow sky?
She jays the water with violet hair
and face and comes up above it
from her waist, chest green with
strikes of wave. Her orange tail
bears two toes. She has no fingers,
but why would she need them?
She has arms, like two pieces
of roses against the brilliant sky.

Water chops around her, and she
smiles. Nothing matters but her arch
up from the sea. It's good to know
waves can't reach the sky. There is
a line, except with her, where she has
splashed, one salty crest, breaking
the horizon to green behind her.
She doesn't really mind.

She curves color. She smiles
from where all waves wish they
could meet with sky. Where she
has come from, and where she will
go, if she is even real, you can ask,
but we'll never need to know.

Stained Glass

Silver salt stains into amber.
Virgin to the north
under the zodiac in the rose,
we have read your instructions
(yes fire, yes burn). Windows
tell stories across the walls.

Orion's sword begins life.
Stars brew like glass, copper
to ruby, manganese to purple,
cobalt to blue. Iron makes
green, sweetness and light.
Blow, cut, slit, press,

my bone, my schist Venus.
We work under you.
Blue supergiants' elements
get heavier in the core
until they reach iron and cave in,
and so of course we fear.

We read the stain, the heavy
burn, as iris unfurling face
and bells. Let us all be full
of grace. Night falls like always
in marble cascade. The sun pushes
to morning. Then it cools.

The Steel My Father Sharpened

He has replaced the bolt, and that is all.
The hand shovel I held as a child, too large
for my grip then, fits me now. The steel
digs, dark and ample. The wood handle
is polished slick from our oil, our sweat,
our palms' pressure applied to the earth
these thirty-odd years.
                        Today, from what
my son calls lambstone, from this sandstone,
limestone, the bones of an old sea,
I hold the stems of fire pink, silene virginica,
while my father separates out grass and weeds
from scarlet parts and shallow roots that have
learned to thrive in rocky soil.
                        Our guild
receives these ways of dirt, blade, and wood,
my son my father's namesake, sileni, these sons
of wine. They break apart root from root
with solid same hands. The clod opens to air.
I watch my father and son break it down.

At the East of the Garden

A small fire burns under the tree, a hurry
of sharp flames that flash like hours. Owls
call in patterns that we don't know, proud,
burdened as men who present their city
of metals and stones, occasional marble,
corners which bear names. Gargoyles
pour unseen above the many engines. A city
holds the shade of mushrooms, not of the tree
or fire, even in cathedrals' uttering, the pulse
in any bell, in the tunnels. The refinery
flames, like swords, are polished into shining.
The city mushrooms low to the ground
in a haze, and above it, stands the tree,
under which there is a small fire burning.

Grandchildren of Other Summers

Pipevine, spicebush—
swallowtails fill the four abelias
by my father's road.

One-hundred butterflies,
grandchildren of other summers,
move as if the night sky

were wound tight:
orange globes in triple-digit heat,
the blue just off the moon's edge,

the black of deep space
where nothing returns
to the eye.

One hundred, my son
and father declare,
standing in the road

together, seventy
years apart. I lost
count at thirty-five.

Purple String

The bride with the purple string around her head
was the child of a father who didn't care she wasn't
a son, that he never had a son, that his name ended
even after all fathers had carried it before. She wore
the purple string, that there would be a throne
of white wood inside a dark and balanced place,
the center of a house low to the ground
where air sweeps stone as it enters.

He thought she was a powerful child, not to be
a king, but full of song like air and water. She moved
through the right angles of city blocks
broken by post oaks and hydrangeas,
past the numbers of houses counted out
like money or time. She called him
by his first name, like a friend.

Since bad spirits travel in straight lines,
she took the purple inside her hair
like the curves off the sides of lightning
that branched as trees from limb
to limb, so that their dreams
might all be better.

Don't leave. Stay here forever, said the father

to the air
in her eyes, her mouth, between her fingers,
the web between thumb and index finger
that as a child, she was afraid
she might cut with scissors,
that soft rose
that made her a girl,
not a sparrow
of the dawn, not an arrow
cut from viburnum
and smoothed with an easy wrist
in the hands of a master.

Don't leave. Stay here. She will not
bear the tray, the silver
beaten to a platter
in the desert
of his mind, the water of the Jordan
like the garden
of God, the fords
of slaves and kings, promises
of brass and the head of the axe
floating.

Stay here. Forever silver,
border
and meander
to the dead sea, which has no outlet, metal
to turn the hearts of fathers
to their children
before the face to prepare
their ways. The curse
of the earth,

the arrival
from the barren, is born
from what can't speak.

All One

Her shadow pressed to the ground
as leaves scratched in drought. The monarch
heading south flattened on the forest floor.
Come another wave, cold and long.
It passed to the woods, which pulled in again
with lungs. Hold on, she told herself,
to what you know: wood and leaves
sound like water and sand on a shore;
leaves leave without a word; wood turns
until it breaks and falls; a shadow doesn't turn
but keeps to the opposite side of the sun
no matter which way a body walks or runs.
Is this what it means to drown? Hush,
said the air. You can open your eyes now.

And Hope to Die

Bud I love,
lilac, red

on the edges, like pain,
you color so colorful.

His favorite color
is blue

which you will turn
into. Sir.

So this is where
your heart is, forward

in the forest, which grows
closer to the edge of your house

daily. I swear
(cross my heart).

The drop in your eye
doesn't help you see,

not blue, not anything
(no one can say why),

nor do you remember
the lilac, or blue.

Father. The eyes part
like a bud in the gap

between word and color,
the red edge of blue.

Particle, Little Part

She ran to the forest like the women before her,
and like them, she turned into a tree that the gods
gave her name, a way to honor a woman, an object
of desire. She multiplied into woods that crews cut
and set on fire in their hurry to build wider roads
between the cities so that people could drive faster,
safer. The piles of timber on the shoulders burned
for a solid week until what was left hung in the air
as if suspended in limbs that no longer existed
and then caught in the lungs of those sensitive,
the elderly, the children. People took medicines
to keep cells from dividing, prayed to god
to be better, to win the battle inside them.
The cities issued guidance about breathing.

Of the Air

The man couldn't decide between meadow and prairie
so he called the bird sparrow
and took a break by moving on to mammals
as they seemed easier,
what with their fur and large eyes of oil.
The sparrows left that part of the garden
and began creating subspecies,
all of them singing.

To make the man return to sparrows, the god gave verses
about hair and farthings,
which the man heard, not as money, but a thing far from him,
like a city or another planet. He named those for love,
or war, depending on how he was feeling, see, he could name
much more than the living. The sparrows
blinked bits of coal
with third eyelids that were concealed.

American Robin

The robin of satin is rapture,
is like the motion of soil, furnace red
underneath like coal on fire,
sunset.

The robin turns its head
to listen,

its crescent eye
a moon in coal, an appetite
in violets
named for the foot of the bird,

a steady eye
in crushed limestone.

The front porch underneath
has been painted blue, as if sky (not
wood), as if eggshell
left broken

in front of the house
on the ground.

The morning after a storm,
you can hope a robin was born
but should know better
the rapture

of a storm at night, a coal
vein torn.

What is left
underneath the open shell
soaks in the soil. The robin
turns its head to listen.

Marigold

Tell me the valley was yellow every other morning.
Some would say gold, but I know the color
as the sun come back from night once more and full
of promise. It was the moment right at the second
when the light bent around the horizon
then changed, as light will and does.
Is this a river valley? Or one of many creeks?
On the prairie, or the hills where the last glaciers
never reached? Yes. Think school bus yellow running roads
with children inside half asleep except for those dreaming.
Think marigolds that we planted in vegetable gardens
to control pests but also, for the hidden reason,
beauty. Think of all the flowers of the gardens that few notice
because we long for the end, not realizing
how the bloom folds around itself into the fruit it bears,
what we share with each other, the harvest
always more than we can use, more than we can keep.

Oh Be a Fine God, Kiss Me

Stars, sand, sons
in motion, spin.
The little girl sings:

what pulls the salmon?
what pulls the bunting,
indigo as belief?
who can count the sand?
the stars? Naked eye,

the ocean sky, it grinds
hard stone to sand,
more stars in a spectrum of heat
(believe), more sons.

The little girl sings.
Even as I sleep
flat on my back,

they turn, a wheel
of sand, in patterns,
each one unfolding
to the bluest heat.
They never speak, not even

of you who bent to my face
and gave me a taste,
gave them to me.

First the Bats, Then the Stars

Fingers and thumb wring into wings. The bats
echolocate as whales and dolphins hunting
through new stellar loops. Corona, corolla,
core, we sink into more, across cotton from the delta,
along the wine space of mouths. Grapes mass
into oak-wrapped drink. Fibers unlock and spin.
We, love, we begin again. Will we come
up through hands that quiver with the pulses
of star fields? Will we come along the river,
her oxbows flooded with spring? Light, bright
as looking glass, limbs stroke tonight. I would do
most anything, as fur and star in agitation.

Morphology

Give her the name of the longest river in the world
or call her river. Either way, she will collect and hold
and move everyone from one place to another.
You will look into her sometimes and see the sky
above your bodies. You will note if she is dirty,
or running low, or out of control, that the worst
thing for a woman. What luxury, to name one child
for a river so that the rest of the girls can grow up
to measure themselves against her. You develop
her mouth into a harbor and dredge it to be deeper.
Your errors: not to realize the effects of your burning
on the weather, to assume that she will run
like you want her. You will build levees that you expect
to last forever. She never looks over her shoulder.

Quartz Crystal

On the north shore
of the Ouachita,
the landing is flooded
where a mountain bluebird
hovers and sings. Too
far east to be here,
the guidebook reads.
Pay that no mind.

I, a ghost, was sweeping
the south stairs. You were
quartz crystal sold at the fair.

Lady Ghost Lane
connects with no town.
In the winnowed
first fields of hay, damp
undersides lift from stubble
to dry. We drive,
our hands out our windows
like minor wings.

Old sea poured into mountains
born of folds and faults
and was pressed with heat
to change in time.

Butterflies kettle
in the mud. The monarch
leaps in its tiger ways
with kerosene flames
down these old logging lanes.
Rockhounds pry and chisel

the sea's crystal veins, pulling
out prisms to heal all blame.

Translucent, I could only
be pierced by an arrow
built from your stone.

A Cameo Cut in Shell

Desire, my mother like fire,
freckled in the shell,
orange tiger
on the white sugar earth,
impossible soft sugar.
You would fill in your teeth,
the gulf of bone,
the gulf of hope
the artist carved in shell.
Through white sugar shell,
I desire, my mother,
soft sugar tiger
on earth freckled with fire,
and the gulf edged with hope
is an hour in each angle,
is the bone in each angel
that worked cutting the shell.

Charm, Company, Trembling

What is a song but trembling grass
held in the mouth, the flush
of fever, blood pressure, the outline
of a hand on a cave wall?

With hematite, manganese,
I would draw
with purple that shade
of the pomegranate,
of the underworld,
tracing a charmed hand.

I have added the swallowed sounds
of straw stacked to the eaves of barns,
the red eye close to the ground.

I have filled myself with the seeds
of elms (all with wings).

Like an emperor, the pine
stands in the Latin word of crimson.
The berries stain the tongue
just so, the edge of want
not yet done
as the tongue connects to the mouth,
connects to the song.

The stars tremble
so that you know.

II

Story

I know a story of bone built around a ghost,
old seafoam.
I know a raincrow that never calls,
brown and odd.

       It eats the caterpillars that eat the oaks,
its stomach full of their spines,
black spines in its black bill
but never with sound.
       It flies into the story of the bone
without a sound, hanging on the wall
and never keeping time,
ghost in a clock.

I know a story of a stripped oak,
brown and cold.
The raincrow sheds the lining of its stomach
right on time.

Enthalpy

She grips the ice by its fingers,
her skin slipping on its skin
until she learns to use her nails
to catch hold. She can see
her hands through the ice
but blurred as if moving, a screen
from a movie, scene slowed down
so shades drag into watercolors.
When she kisses the ice, her tongue
ripples with its surface. To lick
means knowing the rhythm
of the air when the water froze,
that instant. Both open to a time
one phase of matter shifted
to another. And what are you?
she asks herself, counting digits
until the heat of her fingertips
makes water return again.

Catoptromancy

When all the words had become mirrors,
she looked in and found the afternoon shimmering
like a plain where red-winged blackbirds
wrote liquid notes to one another.
She hung in the gap
between what she could forget
and what she could remember. The children
were picking up sticks that had fallen that winter
for burning. If a mirror cracked,
she would hear them laughing as they worked
to stack bits of every kind of oak
and also wild cherry together
to form a new tree at the center of the garden.
It came alive with flames in the evening.

Green Snake

Asleep in the afternoon, such heat is unclear,
as if the winter's flame under the faucet
grew. That single spot lit to keep the pipes
from freezing when the power was out,
a candle waxed onto the drain, swells
and consumes everything.

The ceiling fan spins a burned flower
through air thick and still, like sluggish creeks.
It might build to afternoon clouds that coax
the sky to rain. On the living room floor
under spinning blades, I forget anything
but such a chance.

After sleep, I walk out, barefoot into
the yard's erratic cut of grass. I step
on the hose my mother uses to pull
water from the well to wash our clothes.
It slides away, across my arch. Green snake,
you'd better run.

You have a weedy skeleton, and my grandmother
has already shown she will hack all snakes apart
with the garden hoe. My father argued
she should leave them alone, but she grew up
in other days, of keeping a stick of wood
by the back door

to push the snakes away, of children seen
not heard, of rods not spared. Sometimes
we find shed snake skins. They have crawled out,
after a thoughtful spell, their new scales
so bright across their length, healing, surging
as if heaving heat.

I won't tell them you were here for a week
at least. For this, work for me new feet
of scales and an underside that measures
waves through earth, of fault lines, footsteps,
the whirring, sharpened blades that keep
all close.

In the city where a woman studies wings,

the fires of refineries along the river
burn almost red, tall as a story
although there's no easy way to judge scale.
Production is good again, and summer
being what it is, we could burst into flame.
Will this summer ever end? Our mothers
ask this every year, not speaking to us
or each other but to the air.

The woman works on the south side
of the city, counting feathers
on each butterfly wing, collectively a fire
metallic blue, not from pigment
but prisms reflecting, like crab shells,
like the buntings' wings bent
past the refineries, come from the south
for summer again and broken into song.

It is the first we've heard of such a thing.
The flare stacks burn what the refineries
vent out so that the air can't catch on fire,
and the size and brightness change
according to the rate of flow. Nights,
the flames grow taller than a man,
a sword, a tongue become a spirit again
that seems to disappear into thin air.

La donna è mobile

The woman is crazy.

You know when they start walking
across fields in rain, across fields
at night, a coyote walking in white

and they can't explain it.

They walk around town when they
haven't walked before, on cracked
sidewalks that end in empty lots.

They wish they could explain it:

a brother must lock her in a room,
a daughter must lock her in a home
where sisters silent in white cotton

walk bright halls, where

doors have alarms. Ina, diminutive,
Celia, blind, still, tied in chairs,
make no mistake, behind their face

(and they can't explain it)

they are walking in their mind, feet
in furrows, across the cracks of mothers'
backs, feathers on landscapes,

and they wish they could explain it.

They change in tone and thought,
like Main Street, wasting away,
and at this time, do not lie.

Equal Shine

I watched her, a sundial in the sun
in the spaces of the white pine trees.
Afternoons, silence was number one,
her kitchen timer ticking by her knees.

Nothing else, no book or radio,
no sunscreen, water, or even open eyes.
I must be quiet or I must go.
She flipped when the timer hit its chime.

Sweat crept like me around her bands,
the old bikini frayed as rough grass.
She didn't sleep, she didn't fan her hands.
The timer clicked the afternoon to brass.

I tried to read a book nearby, burning
my skin trying to be close,
flipping pages quieter than wings
or else, or else, I knew or else.

She adored the sun like a man,
flat, still under his long hot span.
The more time with him, the darker she became.
More time with him, the sharper her face.

A couple of hours seemed so long.
I watched the butterflies in the pines.
I watched her legs burnish into bronze.
I longed to polish mine to equal shine.

Witch Hollow Road

Apples
not grown in a cave valley
are blessed:

trees in rows, cut low
in management, like great roses

from which we can eat,
no fallow dream,
but sweet

as if from a witch's hand
(don't you know that story?),
as if from our common mother's hand
(you know that story, too).

She misses us with her kiss
lost in air.

Rowing in Eden

the prairie sea became wheat,
became luxury,
and you are never done with coal
in the heart of coal country.

Your father says we can't leave
and so we drive
no farther than Sparta
to the west

past peach orchards,
stone, pits, mines, the cemetery
with its angel eyes
where we have never gone

in the middle of the night
to see her sudden glowing sight,
past bars which are too wild
for good girls like us,

coming back to Eden.
Have I told you my father
was born out east on the sea?
Not in this wheat, like us,

which cuts. Not on these rails,
which thrum with coal
in speed. Not in this place's past,
a runaway slave's nights

by the star sea, the compass star.
Not on prairies, wheat or stripped,
lost or flat, not on the river
called Mary.

Your father says we shouldn't leave
and so we drive
above toxic waste dumps
about which no one speaks,

past as many churches as bars,
almighty father in the good book,
good girls, always,
never wild or bad at heart.

I have looked at the map:
in Eden,
we are almost equidistant
from the seas.

Maidenhair

Our radiant maidenhair tree
with seeds soft
and bitter

stands under men who dive out
of planes from Hunter Field.
They glide over

the steam shovels and coal gondolas
around Sparta and the old
strip mines

of boulders, over soybean rust
and dry glacial plains.
We watch them

bloom from seeds to parachutes
of delicate red. Our ginkgo
grows

a thick crown, a rocket of fossil
through chaff, coal dust,
ash,

and diesel, great limbs reaching.
The men land from the sky
and drive away.

So Eden sank to grief

as any place with streets that assume that trees
are equal to men, streets crossed by Spring,

Church, Crown,
at the end of which a tall house is falling

where carpet once was rolled out
to confuse bloodhounds

chasing runaway slaves, now long gone, brick,
Greek Revival, with old TV antenna, down. Eden sank

in walnut and vines,
the first four presidents still on street signs

past bulldozed city blocks, a basketball goal,
a few homes of chain smoke,

satellite on all night and the shades drawn.
At the other end of Crown,

the first person we really knew from birth
slept on a quilt spread on the floor,

baby in gold afternoon hours
with lips subsiding into dreams. Upon

earth's face, we watched her sleep,
one of us on either side, speaking

over her in low tones. Upon earth's face,
she woke in grief.

A Good Pair of Scissors, if Taken Care of, Will Last You Forever

Where is the mother, heavy
with all she remembers?
The shallow drawer for spools of thread,
honest colors without names,
shades to match any piece of clothing;
another drawer, deep, with patterns,
women drawn with legs from here
to there, ordered by numbers;
then the drawer of odds
and ends, silver shears
never to be used on anything
but fabric, pin cushions
shaped as tomatoes, perfect
red in the palm and all the pins
the daughter rearranges
in patterns, as constellations
or silver flowers to please her.
Have you been in here
again without my permission?
Have you touched my scissors?
The child has seen her eyes
in the blades, which she has
not touched but imagined
in her hair, in construction paper,
in the garden, the slide
of two knives working together,
almost dancing, whatever
has been cut, falling away.

Graeae, What We Share

We wander, sisters,
across the majority of the earth.
In the foam, we share one eye
as good women,
one vision with depth
of all zones,
through marine snow,
past the abyss.

Born with one eye, with hands
that know how to lock
and pass without seeing, with skin
that knows sight
and voices that don't
need anything but one
tooth, again shared,
a bone bared,

we roam, graeae
in lunar rhythms.
What does gravity know
of the bodies of swans
or the arms of old women
who have born all: hope,
fear, love, the wrap around
oneself when alone,

the rocking to say
you are not alone.
We remember our mother's pace
as we bloomed in her womb,
she of sharks

and whales, she
who knew rocks
and war. Wrapped

in saffron, terrible,
sometimes destroyer,
she wore the sun's
gold stigma, stalk, and style dried
and ground to richness, love
as pleasure in crocus
dust. Sisters, she
showed us the way.

Before the Garden Door, Shimmering Light

Red threads her hair like a cardinal,
an initial, a lesser known law
about the right way of thought.
She bends where she has often walked,
where her daughter feels she can't go,
lilies, marigolds, rose, heads of peonies
that nod down as soon as they open,
too heavy with beauty to remain
upright. In this place, she spends hours
at a time on her knees. The town
continues in its ritual of trucks and baseball
across the highway, boys only,
and her daughter is often watching.

Still Life with Apples

The seven girls,
like stars, like red
and gold desire, aged
no less than seventeen
and no more than twenty,
inhale as they take
the stage, sponsored

by the local Dairy Queen,
by abstract
and title companies.
Of good moral character,
they have never birthed a child,
never divorced
or married. They exhale

like stars in evening
gowns, wishing
for that scholarship,
second runner up, first,
each sister in turn. Acres
of air are born of red June
and Rome beauty.

The seven change
to doves, then stars, to calm
the fathers watching
in the middle-school auditorium,
fathers who think
they can give them nothing
but this opportunity.

Another Man Who Lost His Head

After permission slips, the railroad man
shows us the video, the lights in the library
turned low. I can't see the bodies meant
to scare us straight. The shots are too dark,
like root cellars, canned beets wet in the corner,
always eaten last, and not as real as afterbirth
or the innards of deer, steaming in winter.

They tried to beat the train, and that's
his head off in his girlfriend's lap, he taps
the glass. Some girls croon gross. We know
the rules and aren't so stupid to say otherwise.
Trains stop us every day, often going backwards
through town halfway, the bells in urgent red,
crossing loving arms over the coal. Sometimes
the dark will play tricks on your mind.

The galaxy hung between the girl and her mother

like a brooch in the air, smudge, haze, spiral
on a core they once knew. Her mother sat
in her chair, more lovely
than the sea. The girl was all legs
across the northeast horizon, in bed early
like the children in the city
now that the time had changed, falling
back in fall so that it got dark
early, and like the children, she wasn't
yet sleeping, head full
of thoughts, the kind that keep a girl,
not a child or woman, up all hours. The star
called the head of the chained woman
was the same as the one called the horse's navel,
horse born from the beheading
of his mother, a spring
of wings before suddenly flight.
Her mother rested in her chair, looking
at the inside of her eyes.
The center of the horse connected to the girl's mind
with all its deep space objects:
quintet, cluster,
spirals, ellipses, and a cross
in which a galaxy forms a lens
across a quasar,
gravity bending the light.

Everything will be splendid: the grandmother will not drink habitually

and they will walk through the Jewel Box, leftover
from a depression, glass that resists the fracture of hail. Out
into canna lilies, carmine, flames, like the ones she once set
out in her garden, her words won't cross and she will
remember her garden and what is clear will be water,
as the glass of the box in its green frame. This third time

will be a charm. She will sleep with the shell of the moon
above her, not away the best part of the day. She will
wear old rhinestones, necklace and matching brooch
loud as cannas, the rhizome set in full sunlight as a wish,
and she will smile into a story as a child into a jewel box,
a reflecting pool echoing her face. She won't break.

Elegy

In the water, a serious reflection:
her face drawn into sky
without clear features,
as if eyes, nose, mouth, mean nothing
even after all that practice.
An infant thinks it a game
to learn those words, and adults
say no different. But here the child
finds herself a blur. The pasture
waves around her, once prairie,
now barbed wire between the house
and this stockpond, an eye
men cut with a backhoe
so the cattle would never go thirsty.
Laundry whips on the clothesline
as two halves of bodies drying
again and again in her and her parents'
sizes. She touches her face.
It seems the pieces are still,
but the water says never.
A red-tailed hawk circles,
followed by flame.

Learning Latin in Sparta

Agricola, farmer was the first word
and after that came the terms for war.

My parents have chosen two options:
the parts of the body, the parts of law.

From the egg to the apples, I hold
a wolf by the ears. We learn the history

of a dead empire across the sea, not
of our place here: this town first

named Columbus, for the man
who discovered this world, before men

met at a general store and chose
a new name, Sparta, a bricktown of coal.

We decline, we derive, from cotton
and castor beans and the railroad from

St. Louis to Cairo. A runway runs so close
to Pizza Hut, it has a light that strobes.

I'm bad with names of generals
but hold to stories, like the opal,

now bad luck, once precious in Rome.
It is my grandmother's name. Bonus,

bona, bonum, like her, I try
whiskey alone. An eagle doesn't eat flies.

Soil folds around the crop rotations.
We fit personal endings to verb forms.

Raptor

The child mistakes an angel for a hawk
as deer cross the moon in city yards.
Its phase has struck her parents
in different ways: her mother counting errors,
a variety of buttons, into a wide-mouthed jar,
her father never looking in mirrors. Hard-pressed,
the deer move in the perimeter they know. The fur
behind their ears has gone black with winter
so that, with a quick glance, they all seem horned.
They have dug for acorns until their flesh is sweet.
The child counts buttons like gems drilled

through with holes, leftovers from coats and shirts
and small bags attached to what was new. She draws
on the mirror when no one looks, always
the same two eyes, dot nose, and smile.
The flame of flight, a sweep of rust, then white;
a body that goes up in smoke hunting
songbirds at the feeders at dawn: the hawk again,
the child reports. Her mother shakes the jar
to make the circles shift. Her father wishes so hard
that he could fly that he can taste the words.
Even in the city, the morning is a bird.

Snake, Not Serpent; Hopelessness, Not Despair

We shouldn't use Latinate words,
too many syllables, abstractions, flowers.
Instead, use words with Germanic roots,
shorter, to the point. As if half our tongue
was wrong. As if flowers, too,
didn't belong. Oh, you know what I mean.
Yes, I do: erase those empires and the gods. Say fall,
not autumn; ghost, not phantom;
drought, not famine; fire, not flame.
We have aches, not pains, graves, not tombs.
As if no one from such places
could speak of concrete things,
as if no one came here from such places at all.
Like immigrant. Say one who comes.

Waterweed

Elodea, my soft trousseau, fills green threes
        in water, floating from fragments of fall.
With cytoplasmic streaming, it breaks and roots
        again, such cloth of gold in the longest trains
from lake bottoms. Susceptible is love, on stems
        and tips in silt. We were first made
from stone and then from trees, but we left
        such stories as shores for dusty breath.
Eve had no mother, starting new like lonely bone
        from a stranger's side. The water teems
with green that absorbs light in leaves two cells thick.
        Gold filaments run the silk with warp and weft
as three leaves through water. I rise as white
        bloom on the surface where air exchanges
with liquid, where marry is triplets of notes
        on clefs of depth and shimmer
with no aisle but the steady, daily sun. I wrap
        in fluid sheen and break and root again.

NOTES

Many thanks to the editors and staff of the following journals in which poems in this collection first appeared, sometimes in slightly different form:

2River View "Maidenhair"

Adanna "Waterweed"

Arts & Letters "So Eden sank to grief"

Bear Review "A Good Pair of Scissors, if Taken Care of, Will Last You Forever"

Bluestem "Oh Be a Fine God, Kiss Me," "Quartz Crystal," "Story"

Bone Bouquet "American Robin"

Cave Wall "Equal Shine"

The Cincinnati Review "Stadium Effect"

Cold Mountain Review "Enthalpy"

The Common "Snake, Not Serpent; Hopelessness, Not Despair"

Connotation Press.com "Breakers," "Dame's Rocket"

Cream City Review "Learning Latin in Sparta"

Cumberland River Review "Green Snake"

DIAGRAM "Purple String," "Rowing in Eden"

Folio "La donna é mobile"

Glass: A Journal of Poetry "Graeae, What We Share"

Hampden-Sydney Poetry Review "Raptor"

Heron Tree "Witch Hollow Road"

Inkwell "Trailing Point"

Jet Fuel Review "The galaxy hung between the girl and her mother"

The Laurel Review "Everything will be splendid: the grandmother will not drink habitually"

Louisiana Literature "At the East of the Garden," "Still Life with Apples"

The Louisville Review "All One"

The MacGuffin "Marigold"

Naugatuck River Review "Grass Domes"

NELLE "Iron Is Red When You Put Water on It"

New Orleans Review "First the Bats, Then the Stars"

Nimrod International Journal "Grandchildren of Other Summers"

The Pinch "The Steel My Father Sharpened"

Quiddity "Charm, Company, Trembling"

Redactions: Poetry & Poetics "Marcescence"

RHINO "Elegy"

Salamander "Morphology," "Particle, Little Part"

South Dakota Review "Don't leave. Stay here forever, said the father," "In the city where a woman studies wings"

Southern Women's Review "In the Labyrinth of the Smallest Bone"

Sou'Wester "Catoptromancy"

Spoon River Poetry Review "Breaking the Horizon to Green Behind Her"

Stoneboat "A Cameo Cut in Shell"

Sugar House Review "Conclave," "Of the Air"

Terrain.org "Stained Glass," "Sunset Cue"

Third Coast "And Hope to Die"

Waccamaw "Another Man Who Lost His Head," "While the wren sings, the heron flying across the lake"

Yemassee "Before the Garden Door, Shimmering Light"

Zone 3 "Star Witness, a Moth"

"So Eden sank to grief" takes its title from Robert Frost's "Nothing Gold Can Stay." "Rowing in Eden" takes its title from Emily Dickinson's "Wild Nights - Wild Nights!" "La donna é mobile" takes its title from Giuseppe Verdi's *Rigoletto*. "Everything will be splendid: the grandmother will not drink habitually" takes its title from Louise Bogan's "Evening in the Sanitarium." "Before the Garden Door, Shimmering Light" takes its title from Édouard Vuillard.

"Catoptromancy" was featured June 4, 2020, and "Stadium Effect" on March 10, 2021, at *Verse Daily*.

ACKNOWLEDGMENTS

Special thanks to the Arkansas Arts Council for an individual artist fellowship, Melissa Gill for a sensational image for the cover, and Nicholas Grosso, Joey Nicoletti, Jennifer Martelli, Maria Terrone, and Bordighera Press and the John D. Calandra Italian American Institute for awarding this book space.

I appreciate all my friends and family who brought me to a place where I could write and value these poems, especially Phillip, Tanutda, Cheryl, and Becky, for being some of the first to care what I was trying to say; the students at Pulaski Technical College and Hendrix College, who shared time, grit, and dreams; my grandfather Rocco, who couldn't understand much but music by the time we were together but smiled at me to play; and my grandmother Angelina, who died twenty years before I was born, from whom I inherited my name. I carry part of you with me always.

And to our Team D-M-H, Wade, Sidra, Jude, Jack, and Clementine, who encouraged me to return to these poems during the pandemic to pull this book together as a way to find meaning despite, or through, the chaos: you are everything to me.

ABOUT THE AUTHOR

ANGIE MACRI was born and raised in southern Illinois, where her mother's family has lived for more than two centuries. Her father's family comes from Calabria by way of Seattle, Washington, and Brooklyn, New York: her grandfather was born in Roccella Ionica, and her grandmother's parents were born in Longobucco. Her first book *Underwater Panther* (Southeast Missouri State University) won the Cowles Poetry Book Prize. An Arkansas Arts Council fellow, she lives in Hot Springs.

ABOUT THE COVER ARTIST

MELISSA GILL is a printmaking and textile artist, and an educator. Her work portrays an intricately balanced environment where the borders between subject and background are shifting and permeable. She is currently Professor of Art at Hendrix College and a faculty member of the Arkansas Museum of Art.

LAURIA/FRASCA POETRY PRIZE

The prize was conceived to promote the poetry of the Italian diaspora in English. Quality poetry in any style and on any theme is sought.

MATTHEW CARIELLO. *Talk*. Vol. 1. 2018
JANET SYLVESTER. *And Not to Break*. Vol. 2. 2019
JANINE CERTO. *Elixir*. Vol. 3. 2020 (Copublished with New American Press)

www.ingramcontent.com/pod-product-compliance
Lightning Source LLC
Chambersburg PA
CBHW030050100426
42734CB00038B/1075